Gabrielle
and the Fossil Hunt

Gabrielle H. Lyon with Joyce Goldenstern

Contents

Rigby.

Chapter 1
An Invitation to Explore

A huge dinosaur **claw** lay on a rock. We began digging to see if we could find more of the dinosaur. Suddenly a sandstorm circled around us and blew sand in our eyes. We covered our heads but kept digging. After a while, we found a dinosaur **skull** with a long jaw and many teeth. The teeth looked like they belonged to a **crocodile.** I was tired and my eyes stung, but I was thrilled! I knew then, in 1997, that I wanted to share this exciting discovery with kids. So when I returned home from this dinosaur hunt in Africa, I helped plan a new science organization for kids called Project Exploration.

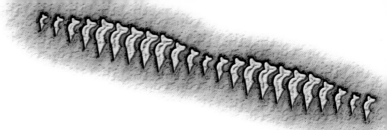

My name is Gabrielle Lyon, and I am the director of Project Exploration. I am also an **expedition** team member, which means that I go on long trips all over the world to search for dinosaur fossils. I would like to invite you to follow me on another dinosaur hunt and learn about **paleontology,** which is the study of **fossils** and ancient life.

I was looking for dinosaur bones during a trip for my organization, Project Exploration.

What Do Paleontologists Do?
- They study and describe animal and plant fossils.
- They clean and repair fossils.
- They study how life changes over time.

Why We Go to Africa

In the year 2000, I went back to Niger, a country in Africa, to look for more bones of the crocodile-like dinosaur and other fossils. All of our trips to Niger are important because most of the dinosaurs that scientists know about so far have been found in North America and Asia, not in Africa. Our team wanted to study how dinosaurs around the world are alike and how they are different.

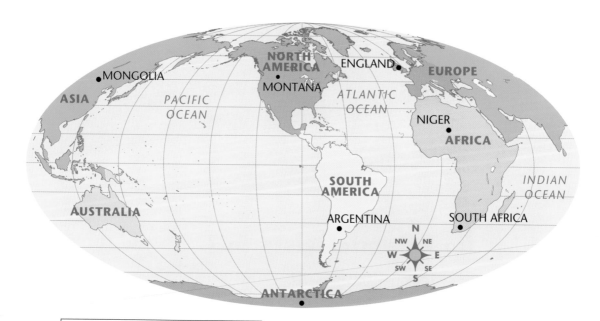

Key:
• = dinosaur fossil sites

On this trip, we also wanted to return a dinosaur skeleton to the people of Niger. When we find fossils in other countries, we study, repair, and make copies of them in our lab in the United States, but then we must return them. We were bringing back the fossil bones and the skeleton of a huge, plant-eating dinosaur called *Jobaria,* which we had discovered during our trip in 1997. This dinosaur lived 135 million years ago!

Jobaria Skeleton

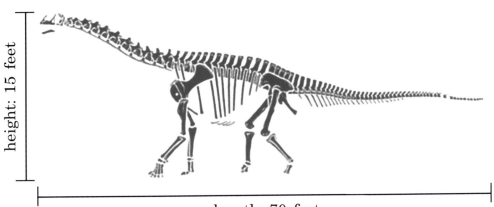

height: 15 feet

length: 70 feet

Planning Our Trip

Because we would be in a desert called the Sahara for a 4-month trip, we needed many things. Since we wouldn't have a refrigerator, we brought dried food that didn't need to stay cold. We brought a lot of pasta, rice, dried meats, vegetables, and even powdered milk. (It was enough food to feed 14 people for 4 months!)

We brought water jugs to fill at wells in the desert and freeze-dried ice cream, which is stored in a package with no air. Freeze-dried food doesn't spoil, so it can be eaten for a long time.

We brought dried foods such as pasta and rice on our trip.

We also took equipment that we needed for work, including tools for digging up fossils, and cloth and **plaster** for wrapping and protecting them. We brought a computer because part of my job on this trip was to tell young students in Project Exploration about my adventure. I set up a Web site and e-mail so that I could communicate with them everyday. They couldn't wait to hear about Africa!

Paleontologists need different kinds of tools to dig for fossils.

Setting Up Camp

Finally we arrived in Niger, Africa. We set up camp in the desert near a site that we had begun to explore on our trip in 1997. We were sure that we would find many fossils there!

We put up three big tents that became our kitchen, our library, and our storage area. Some team members slept in small tents, but I liked to sleep outside on a cot where I could see the stars.

Here is one of the many tents that was in our desert camp.

During the day the temperature could get up to 120° Fahrenheit or above, but at night the desert was cool. Bright stars filled the sky and looked as if they were dropping all the way down to the ground! It was beautiful!

Because there wasn't much water, we used a small tub and a sponge instead of taking showers when we got up in the morning. We talked about our work for that day while we ate breakfast.

The desert can get as hot as 120° Fahrenheit or higher during the day.

Chapter 2
Looking for Dinosaurs

The dryness of the desert keeps fossils in good condition. But as we looked for fossils, the desert rocks sometimes confused us because they looked like they were bones. Finding a fossil is like trying to find a green lizard on a green leaf. You have to look very closely!

Can you find the green lizard on the leaf?

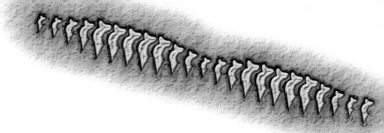

I will tell you how I hunted for bones. I walked around and looked at the ground until I saw something unusual. Sometimes I would see a color that was different from the rocks on the ground. Sometimes I would see the shape of a broken bone. When I saw something interesting, I couldn't wait to take a closer look!

Some team members looked for fossils.

An Exciting Discovery

One day our team returned to the area of the desert where we first found the claw and skeleton of the crocodile-like dinosaur. We saw some backbones sticking out of the ground. It was a new site! We had to be very careful because we did not want to harm these bones. We wanted to see if more bones were under the sand.

We found more bones from the crocodile-like dinosaur.

After we dusted off the bones with a brush, we saw the backbone, the ribs, hand bones, and foot bones of the crocodile-like dinosaur. It was an incredible discovery! Carefully some of us dug up bones, while others rolled the extra rocks away in wheelbarrows. We wrapped the fossils with damp strips of cloth dipped in plaster, a liquid that hardens.

After the plaster was dry, we shipped our discovery to the laboratory at the University of Chicago. At the laboratory, scientists removed the plaster jackets and used brushes, picks, special glue, and drills to clean and repair the fossils. After the fossils are cleaned, repaired, and studied, they would be sent to the museum in Niger.

This paleontologist was using special tools to dig.

13

Chapter 3
Understanding Fossils

We now had a more complete skeleton of the crocodile-like dinosaur and could compare the size and shape of different bones. These bones would help us understand more about this dinosaur. We measured it and found that it was about 36 feet long. We also figured out that this dinosaur lived about 110 million years ago and walked on its 2 back legs.

This paleontologist was studying the claw of the crocodile-like dinosaur.

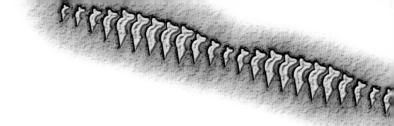

The teeth of this crocodile-like dinosaur are very similar to crocodile teeth.

We examined the teeth and jaws of the fossil, and we guessed that the dinosaur was good at catching fish. This dinosaur was the biggest meat-eater while it lived. We figured this out by comparing its skull to animals today that have the same type of mouth and curved teeth, and we found that all of these animals use their teeth to grab and hold fish. We know this because we know that when the crocodile-like dinosaur was alive, it lived in a wet environment with trees and wide rivers. (We even found fossils of very large fish nearby that lived in these rivers.)

Questions from Kids

Every evening I would write about what the team did that day and e-mail it to the Project Exploration expedition Web site at **www.dinosaurexpedition.org.** Students would e-mail their questions to us.

One student asked how dinosaurs died. Many people ask this interesting question. A lot of scientists believe that a very large rock from space hit Earth and that this changed Earth's climate. They believe that the dinosaurs could not get used to the new climate so they died. No one knows for sure.

Some scientists believe that a very large rock from space killed the dinosaurs.

Another student wondered about the color of dinosaurs. We will never know what color dinosaur skin was because dinosaur skin did not last after the animal died. But we can study living reptiles to get an idea of what dinosaur skin might have looked like.

We can look at living reptiles like turtles, lizards, and snakes to help us guess what color skin the dinosaurs had.

Final Days of Our Trip

After several months of digging, we found amazing bones from many different animals, such as fish, turtles, crocodiles, flying reptiles, and dinosaurs. We were very happy with what we had discovered! Before we left Niger, we traveled to Niamey, the capital city, to set up the skeleton of *Jobaria*. We unpacked the boxes that the bones were shipped in, and we put the skeleton together at the National Museum.

two turtle fossils

long wing finger
of a flying reptile

Here is the skeleton of *Jobaria* at home in Niger.

We waited for the school children to come and see this huge animal. Many of the children had never seen a complete dinosaur skeleton before. *Jobaria* was back in its own country for everyone to enjoy. We were happy for them, but we were sad because our trip was over.

Chapter 4
Encouraging Young Scientists

I loved being a team member looking for dinosaur fossils in Niger, but I also love working with students at home. At Project Exploration, we like to let children experience looking for fossils. Children work together to uncover the bones of a dinosaur. They also have a chance to repair its broken bones, just like we do in our laboratory. After our Niger expedition, we created an **exhibit** at the Chicago Children's Museum about the discovery of the crocodile-like dinosaur.

Project Exploration has an exhibit at the Chicago Children's Museum in Chicago, Illinois.

CHICAGO CHILDREN'S MUSEUM

Sometimes we invite children to come to our lab where we study the fossils that we find on our trips. After the students help us clean the bones, we repair them and sometimes we must make broken and missing bones from plastic in order to build a complete skeleton.

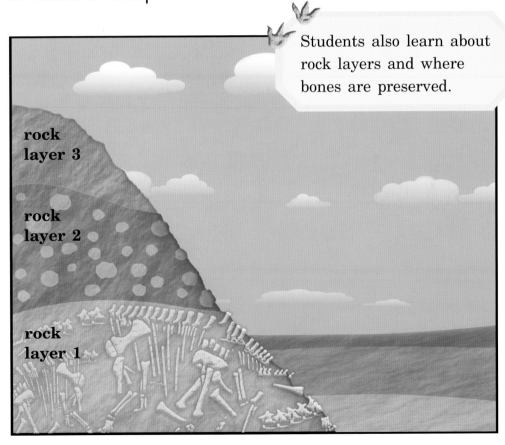

Students also learn about rock layers and where bones are preserved.

rock layer 3

rock layer 2

rock layer 1

Junior Paleontologists

One of the programs we offer at Project Exploration is our Junior Paleontologist program. Each year 12 children from Chicago are chosen to spend 2 weeks learning paleontology skills. Then they travel with scientists to Wyoming or Montana to look for dinosaur fossils.

These kids helped clean dinosaur bones.

Of course, not every student in Project Exploration wants to be a paleontologist, but every student has fun looking for fossils and learning about how science works!

This student, Marco, went on a dinosaur hunt in Montana with Project Exploration.

Glossary

claw a sharp hard part on the toe of an animal

crocodile a reptile with a long mouth and sharp teeth

exhibit a way of displaying information

expedition a long trip made by a group of people to explore something

fossil a part or print of an ancient plant or animal

paleontology the study of fossils and ancient life

plaster a paste mix used to protect fossils

skull a head bone

Index